Queen Elizabeth II's Britain

By Jacqui Bailey

W

Franklin Watts
Published in Great Britain in 2015 by The Watts Publishing Group

Series Editor: Sarah Peutrill
Art Director: Jonathan Hair
Series Designer: John Christopher.

Dewey number: 941'.085
ISBN: 978 1 4451 4222 7

Printed in China

Franklin Watts
An imprint of
Hachette Children's Group
Part of The Watts Publishing Group
Carmelite House
50 Victoria Embankment
London EC4Y 0DZ

An Hachette UK Company
www.hachette.co.uk
www.franklinwatts.co.uk

FSC
www.fsc.org
MIX
Paper from
responsible sources
FSC® C104740

CONTENTS

THE LONGEST SERVING BRITISH MONARCH

Queen Elizabeth II's Diamond Jubilee in 2012 celebrated the fact that she has been on the throne for 60 years. The only other British monarch to rule for longer was Queen Victoria, who reigned for 63 years and seven months, from 1837 to 1901. In September 2015, Elizabeth II will pass this record set by her great-great-grandmother.

Elizabeth came to the throne in 1952, six and a half years after the end of World War II (1939–45). During her reign she has seen many changes that have affected every part of our lives, from the way we eat and dress and the houses we live in, to the jobs that we do and the way we travel. In 1952 computers and mobile phones did not exist. Hardly anyone owned a fridge or a washing machine, let alone a television.

The young Princess Elizabeth waves at the crowds from the balcony at Buckingham Palace in May 1937, after the coronation of her father, King George VI.

ALL CHANGE

Today, we have more choices about the things we can do and buy than at any other time in history. And we can travel in less than a day to places that would have taken our great-grandparents weeks to reach.

This book is a short history of the UK over the past 60 years. It looks at some of the ways in which our homes and lives have changed, including the lives of the Royal Family. Our parents and grandparents will probably remember many of those changes, and perhaps this book will help them to share some of those memories with you, because above all this book is a family history – our own and the Queen's.

The Queen and members of the Royal Family stand on the balcony at Buckingham Palace during the Trooping of the Colour ceremony in June 2010, to celebrate the Queen's official birthday.

Then & Now

A Royal view

Buckingham Palace became the main royal residence in 1837 when Queen Victoria came to the throne, but the most well-known bit of it was only added in 1850 when the large East Front was built facing The Mall. This is the part of the Palace that most people see, and it includes the famous balcony. The first known royal balcony appearance took place in 1851, when Queen Victoria stood there during the opening celebrations of the Great Exhibition. It has since become a tradition for members of the Royal Family to stand on the balcony at times of national importance or celebration.

On the 6th and 9th August 1945, the USA dropped two atomic bombs on Japan. It was the first and only time so far that nuclear weapons have been used in war. The effect was shocking. Thousands of people died in seconds, and thousands more in the weeks and years that followed. On the 15th August, Japan surrendered and World War II came to an end. After six years of war the British people were proud of their victory, but they were also exhausted. Homes and buildings lay in ruins, and food and jobs were in short supply.

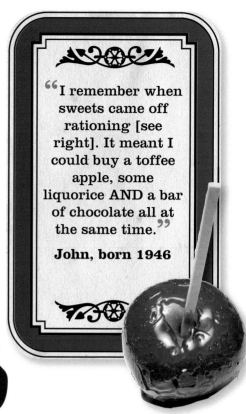

"I remember when sweets came off rationing [see right]. It meant I could buy a toffee apple, some liquorice AND a bar of chocolate all at the same time."

John, born 1946

THE END OF THE WAR

VE Day (for Victory in Europe), on the 8th May 1945, was a day of celebration all over Britain. In the centre of London thousands gathered on the streets, and elsewhere people danced and held street parties. The war in Europe ended when Germany surrendered on the 7th May 1945, and although British troops and others were still fighting in the Far East the news was greeted with excitement and relief in countries across the world.

RATIONING

People's relief that the war was over soon turned to disappointment. During the war basic foods such as meat, eggs, butter, tea, jam, sugar and sweets were rationed. This meant that everyone was only allowed to buy a certain amount of these foods each week.

When the war ended it was hoped that rationing would end too, but it didn't. Instead it carried on for nine more years.

LONDON LAUGHS: By LEE

"A noble fellow, that grocer. Sampling a tin of snoek himself before releasing it to his customers!"

To help with food shortages the government tried to get people to eat a type of canned fish called snoek. It tasted so horrible no one would eat it.

Then & Now

A sweet tooth

During and after the war, sugar was rationed to 340 grams per person per week. That's about 48 teaspoonfuls. Today we eat nearly twice as much sugar, about 560 grams (80 teaspoonfuls) per person per week. Although people do eat more sugary snacks than in the past, there is also sugar hidden in pre-prepared foods.

MARRIAGES AND BIRTHS

In spite of the hardships, most people wanted to get on with their lives. More than 400,000 marriages took place in England and Wales in 1947, and the population increased by more than half a million people due to a record number of births. So many children were born in the years after the war that they became known as the 'baby boom generation'.

Like many other couples in 1947, Princess Elizabeth celebrated the end of the war by getting married to Prince Philip, also known as Lieutenant Philip Mountbatten. And just like those other brides she saved up her clothes rations to buy the material for her ivory satin wedding dress. In 2007, the Queen became the first British monarch to celebrate 60 years of marriage.

A CRUMBLING EMPIRE

At the beginning of the 1900s, the United Kingdom was the richest and most powerful nation in the world. It controlled a vast empire of lands stretching right around the globe, through Africa, Asia, Australia, New Zealand and North America. At the head of this empire was the British monarch – the reigning king or queen.

By the end of World War II, the Empire was crumbling. Countries such as Canada, Australia, New Zealand and South Africa were already governing themselves independently of Britain, although still closely linked to it. In the 1930s they became the first members of the British Commonwealth (now called the Commonwealth of Nations), a group of nations connected to Britain and to each other by their shared interests and values.

THE COMMONWEALTH

After the war, those parts of Africa and Asia still under British control also demanded independence. Gradually most of the nations in Britain's empire became self-governing, although most also chose to join the Commonwealth.

Losing its empire was a blow to Britain's pride, but it no longer had the money or the military power to keep it going and many people felt it was more important to rebuild Britain's wealth at home. Today the Empire no longer exists, although the Queen is still the official monarch of 16 independent countries as well as the UK, and she is currently Head of the Commonwealth, which now has 54 member nations.

The Queen and the Duke of Edinburgh visiting Uganda in 1954. The Queen has been a strong supporter of the Commonwealth throughout her reign, but the next British monarch will not necessarily take over her role as Head of the Commonwealth. The leaders of all of the member countries will decide who the next Head will be when the time comes.

Then & Now

The budget Olympics

The 1948 Olympic Games were the first to be held since before the war and the first to be shown on live television. London was chosen to host the Games and even though there wasn't much money around, George VI felt it was important to go ahead to show Britain's confidence in its future. But there were no brand new Olympic stadiums or other buildings. Instead existing sites around London were used. Athletes were housed in a former army camp in Richmond Park and in RAF camps on the outskirts of London. Nevertheless, 59 nations and more than 4,000 athletes competed and the Games were seen as a great success. London is the first city ever to hold the Olympic Games three times – in 1908, 1948 and in 2012.

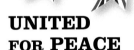 Signs are prepared to help guide the Olympic athletes around their camp site in Richmond Park in 1948. Around 1,500 athletes slept in shared dormitories in the converted army camp.

" All I've done is run fast. I don't see why people should make much fuss about that. "

Fanny Blankers-Koen, (the Dutch sprinter nicknamed 'The Flying Housewife', who won four gold medals in the 1948 London Olympics).

UNITED FOR PEACE

While Britain was unravelling its empire, other nations were banding together – mostly in an effort to avoid another world war. In 1945, the United Nations (UN) came into being, and its first official meeting, or Assembly, was held in London in 1946.

The UK, USA, France, China and Russia (then the Soviet Union) were among the first members of the UN. Today, almost every independent country in the world belongs to the UN, which plays a vital role in keeping the peace, in organising aid when there is a disaster and in helping countries fight poverty and pollution.

A EUROPEAN COMMUNITY

In the 1950s, a group of six European countries also set up the European Economic Community (EEC) – now known as the European Union (EU) – in order to encourage trade between themselves. At the time, the UK did not join the EEC, although it did eventually become a member in 1973.

When Queen Elizabeth was born in 1926 her grandfather, King George V, was still on the throne. Elizabeth's father, Albert, was the King's second son. His older brother, Edward, was heir to the throne so the young Princess Elizabeth did not expect to become queen one day.

Princess Elizabeth (far right) at home with her parents - then known as Queen Elizabeth (later the Queen Mother) and King George VI - and her younger sister, Princess Margaret. The photo was taken in 1938, just a year before the start of World War II.

A NEW QUEEN

KING FOR A YEAR

George V died in 1936 and Elizabeth's uncle became King Edward VIII, but he was never actually crowned. Edward had fallen in love with an American woman called Mrs Simpson who had divorced her two previous husbands. Few people got divorced in the 1930s and the government at the time did not think the British public would ever accept Mrs Simpson as queen. Edward was forced to choose between her and the throne – and he chose Mrs Simpson. In December 1936, less than a year after becoming king, Edward stood down and the throne passed to his brother, who took the name George VI.

THE QUEEN'S FATHER

George VI was a quiet, shy man with a stutter who did not particularly want to become king. But he took his duties seriously and worked hard to support his country and its people throughout World War II and the years that followed. Helped by his wife, George VI earned the respect of Londoners by remaining in London throughout the wartime bombing raids. But early in the 1950s the King became seriously ill and died in February 1952. He was only 56 years old.

Although people loved George VI and were saddened by his death, they welcomed their new queen to the throne. Queen Elizabeth was 25, married with a young family and seemed to represent a new start and a better future after the horrors of the war and the hardships that had followed.

Look out for post boxes with this GR VI symbol (the VI is tucked away in between the initials). This means the box was made during the reign of George VI.

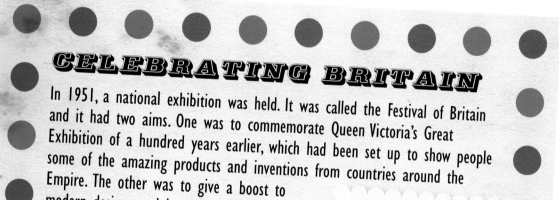

CELEBRATING BRITAIN

In 1951, a national exhibition was held. It was called the Festival of Britain and it had two aims. One was to commemorate Queen Victoria's Great Exhibition of a hundred years earlier, which had been set up to show people some of the amazing products and inventions from countries around the Empire. The other was to give a boost to modern designs and inventions, and to encourage British people to look forward and feel happier and more confident about their future. Events took place all over the country, but a lot were held in London. A special exhibition site was built on the South Bank of the Thames in London and the exhibits there focussed on new scientific discoveries and technological inventions.

Visitors to the Festival of Britain experience a new invention – watching a film in 3-D.

CORONATION DAY

Out of respect for the death of her father (and in the hope of a sunny day), Queen Elizabeth's coronation was held in June 1953, more than a year after she became queen. The ceremony took place in Westminster Abbey in London. Unfortunately it rained on the day, but about three million people lined London's streets to see the young queen drive by in her golden coach.

The Queen insisted that the whole coronation ceremony be broadcast live on television so that everyone could see it as it happened, even though the government was not very keen on the idea. Television was still a very new invention and thousands of people in Britain bought one for the first time just to see the coronation. Friends and family crowded into people's houses to watch on tiny screens. About 20 million people around the world also saw it.

" I was three when the Queen was crowned so I don't really remember the coronation itself, but I do remember sitting in our living room in the dark surrounded by people all staring at a little square box of light at the end of the room. That was the television and we were the first people in our street to have one. "

Sue, born 1950.

Queen Elizabeth in her Gold State Coach, which has been used for every coronation for almost 200 years. It is not made of gold but is covered in layers of gold leaf. It is huge – 3.6 metres high and 7 metres long (nearly as long as a double-decker London bus), and needs eight horses to pull it.

Then & Now

TV times

The BBC began broadcasting television programmes in the late 1930s, but when war broke out in September 1939 television was closed down for security reasons and only BBC radio carried on through the war. As soon as the war was over television started up again, but buying a TV was a luxury few could afford and even by 1955 only about one in three families in Britain had one. Today, virtually every household in the UK has a TV and many homes have more than one.

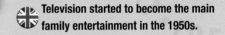 Television started to become the main family entertainment in the 1950s.

OPEN TO THE PUBLIC

All through her reign the Queen has tried to protect royal traditions while also keeping pace with the modern world. She has done away with much of the formality and separateness of the Royal Family, and she and her husband the Duke of Edinburgh have travelled far more than previous monarchs, not only around the UK but also to the Commonwealth countries and other parts of the world. On their travels they try to meet as many members of the public as possible – visiting people in their homes, in factories and hospitals, and on the street.

In 1962, the Queen's Gallery was opened at Buckingham Palace so that people could see some of the paintings and other treasures from the Royal Collection – priceless pieces of art, furniture and other objects collected by British kings and queens over hundreds of years.

In 1993, the Queen allowed the State Rooms at Buckingham Palace to be opened each summer. People queue around the block to visit the throne room, the dining room where the Queen holds state banquets, and the famous balcony (see pages 4–5). A lot of the Queen's other royal houses and palaces are also open to the public.

GOOD TIMES...

The Queen's Diamond Jubilee is not the first celebration of her reign. The Silver Jubilee marking her 25 years on the throne took place in 1977, and the Golden Jubilee for 50 years was held in 2002. On both occasions the Queen spent much of the year travelling to different events around the UK and visiting a number of Commonwealth countries.

> 66 I watched the Party in the Palace on a big screen with thousands of others in Green Park in London. The crowd were singing along to some of the songs, especially the old Beatles' tunes like 'Hey Jude'. 99
>
> **Sarah, born 1973**

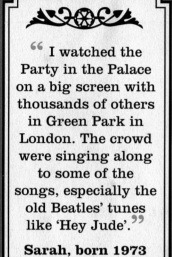

—AND NOW I SUPPOSE THEY'LL EXPECT A DAY OFF FOR **EVERY** JUBILEE!

Thousands of street parties were held in towns and villages all over the country, along with bonfires, firework displays and processions. For the Golden Jubilee in 2002 the gardens of Buckingham Palace were opened up for the first time for a pop concert. About 12,000 people went to the 'Party at the Palace' and millions more watched it on television. A music CD was made of the event and it sold so many copies that the Queen became the first Royal ever to be awarded a gold disc by the recording industry for selling over 100,000 copies of a record.

Crowds gather outside Buckingham Palace during the 'Party at the Palace' for the Queen's Golden Jubilee.

...AND BAD

The Queen and the Royal Family have also had their share of troubles. In 1981 a 17-year-old man fired shots at the Queen as she rode her horse through London during a ceremony. Luckily, the shots turned out to be blanks and the Queen was unhurt.

During the 90s, the British newspapers published stories criticising the Royal Family, and gossiping about the behaviour of some of her children. In 1992, two of her sons, Prince Charles and Prince Andrew, separated from their wives, and her daughter Princess Anne divorced her husband. In the same year a fire broke out at Windsor Castle, one of the Queen's favourite homes, and a large part of the castle was ruined. It took five years to rebuild it. The Queen called 1992 her '*annus horribilus*', her horrible year.

A postage stamp and coin commemorating Charles and Diana's wedding.

THE PEOPLE'S PRINCESS

Most people thought the marriage of Prince Charles to Lady Diana Spencer in 1981 was like a fairytale. The Prince was heir to the throne, and Lady Diana was young and beautiful. At first everything seemed to go well and the couple had two children, Prince William and Prince Harry. But then the marriage started to fall apart and it became obvious that Princess Diana was deeply unhappy. Week after week stories about their marriage appeared in the newspapers and on television. In 1992 Diana and Charles agreed to separate, and then finally divorced in 1996, but to many people in the country she was still 'The People's Princess'. A year after the divorce Princess Diana died tragically in a car crash and most of the country went into mourning. People came in their millions to leave bunches of flowers outside the gates of her home in Kensington Palace and the country almost came to a standstill on the day of her funeral.

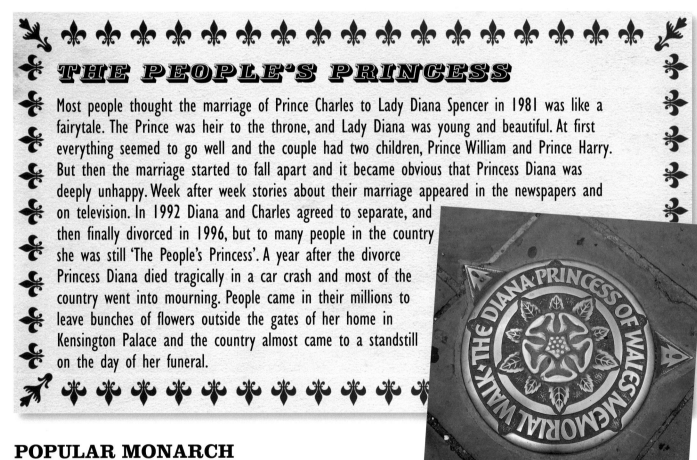

POPULAR MONARCH

In spite of everything, however, the Queen has been a popular monarch throughout her reign and is highly respected for the enormous amount of work she does on behalf of the UK and the Commonwealth. Even so, not everyone agrees with having a king or queen as Britain's head of state. Instead some people would prefer to choose a head of state by popular vote. But for now, most people in the country enjoy having a royal family.

Plaques in the ground mark an 11-kilometre walk from Kensington Gardens to St James's Park in London in memory of Princess Diana.

Britain in the 1950s was a more formal and 'buttoned down' country than it is today. After the upheaval of the war, people wanted to get back to a 'normal' life. For most men this meant having a steady job and a proper home for their wives and families. For most women this usually meant giving up the work they had done during the war and staying at home to look after their husbands and children. The ideal family in the 50s consisted of mum, dad and two or more children.

Prince Charles' marriage to Camilla, Duchess of Cornwall, in 2005 shows how attitudes to divorce have changed over the years. Camilla had divorced her first husband a few years earlier, but Prince Charles was not expected to give up his right to the throne in order to marry her, unlike his great-uncle, Edward VIII, in 1936.

FAMILY LIFE

GETTING MARRIED

Most young people in the 50s and early 60s lived with their parents until they got married. It was shocking and almost unheard of for couples to live together without being married and generally people got married earlier than they do now — usually between the ages of 20 and 24. Today, young people are in no hurry to get married and more than three out of four couples will have lived together beforehand.

More people stayed married in the 50s, too, regardless of how they felt about each other. Divorce was a difficult and expensive process, and it was generally seen as the wrong thing to do. Even so, during the 1960s the number of divorces doubled and in 1969 the law was changed to make divorce easier. About half of all marriages now end in divorce, although many people marry again.

SEEN NOT HEARD

Childhood was also different in the 50s. Children did not have so much attention paid to them as they do today. Instead they were expected to do what they were told and mostly to stay out of the way of adults. Familiar sayings of the time were that children 'should be seen and not heard', and that they should 'speak when they are spoken to or not at all'.

There was hardly any television to watch and no computers or electronic games. Instead most children played outside in the gardens, streets and parks where they lived. They made up imaginary games, or played games such as football, skipping and hopscotch. When it rained they read books or comics, played dice games or card games, or were just bored!

Then & Now

Play time

Not many new toys were made during the war because of the shortage of materials, but by the mid-50s toy manufacturers were back in business. Small metal models of cars, trucks, ships and aeroplanes were hugely popular. The first plastic toys, including 'Lego' and plastic dolls, were also being produced. The first 'Barbie' dolls went on sale in 1959. In the 1970s the first video games appeared in games arcades. One of the most popular was 'Pong' – an electronic version of table-tennis. Computer games arrived with home computers in the 80s. Today, dolls and models are still popular but many children also enjoy electronic games.

> "We used to play out with our friends until it got dark and then we'd all come into one room and listen to the radio – Dick Barton was the thing that was on at about 6 o'clock. He was a special agent. He saved the world many times. It was Dick Barton, Snowy and Jock and there was always a dastardly plot with a cliff-hanger every night."
>
> **Roger, born 1940**

 A normal family meal in 1958, with everyone sitting at the table – and not a television in sight.

SCHOOL DAYS

In the 1930s and early 40s, Princess Elizabeth and her sister Margaret did not go to school. Instead, like the rest of the Royal Family before them, they were educated by tutors coming to their home. Queen Elizabeth and Prince Philip broke with tradition to send their children to fee-paying schools. Prince Charles was the first British heir to the throne to take public exams — then called GCE O-levels and A-levels — and the first to take a degree at university.

🇬🇧 Schools in the 1950s paid a lot of attention to the accuracy of reading, handwriting, spelling and maths. Everyone wore a school uniform, usually a blazer, shirt and school tie, with long or short trousers for boys and skirts or gymslips for girls.

Then & Now

A bottle a day

From 1946 until 1968 every schoolchild was given a third of a pint of full-cream milk to drink at the mid-morning break – whether they wanted it or not. In winter the milk would sometimes be frozen, and in summer was often greasily luke-warm from sitting in the sun. But parents, teachers and the government believed that drinking milk was good for children's health. To save money, school milk was gradually withdrawn, and today only some nursery school children under the age of five receive free milk.

If your parents were wealthy in the 50s they could pay for you to go to a private school. Everyone else went to state schools. Primary school education had been free since the 1890s and in 1944 the Education Act made state secondary schools free as well. The Act also said that all children had to stay at school until at least 15 — before this many left at 14 to go to work.

PASS or FAIL

At the age of 11, children sat an exam called the '11-plus'. If you passed your 11-plus you might get a place at a grammar school. Grammar schools were meant for the cleverest children. You could stay until you were 18 and if you passed your A-level exams could go to university. If you did not pass your 11-plus you would probably go to a secondary-modern school. Secondary-modern schools spent less time on teaching children to pass exams and more on getting them ready to go to work. As well as teaching subjects such as English, maths, history and science, they also taught more practical subjects like woodwork, art, dressmaking and cookery.

"We had a few lessons on computers in my school in the 1980s. They had BBC Bs, which were thought to be the future but were nothing like computers today. They had hardly any memory and a few educational games. You couldn't do any word-processing on them. You had to load the games and they always crashed."

Dan, born 1974

ALL TOGETHER

In most parts of the UK today children no longer have to take the 11-plus. During the 60s and 70s, many people felt it was wrong to divide up children according to whether or not they could pass an exam at such an early age. Instead nearly all grammar and secondary-modern schools were turned into comprehensive schools.

Today pupils must stay at school until they are at least 16, soon to be raised to 18. At 16 they take GCSEs or other types of exams, and can then leave or stay at school for two more years to take A-level exams, diplomas or other qualifications that will help them find a job.

Until 1986 teachers could whack their pupils with a wooden cane or ruler if they behaved badly in school. Then a law was passed banning physical punishment in schools.

Students in 1976 try out some new audio equipment. They are pupils at one of the country's first comprehensive schools, which was built in 1958.

WOMEN'S RIGHTS

Life in the UK became a bit easier in the 60s. There was plenty of work and people began to think less about the war. Instead they were interested in new ideas and were less willing to accept the old, traditional ways of doing things. This was particularly true for women.

Improvements in medicine had led to more reliable forms of birth control, including the contraceptive pill. For the first time women had the power to decide how many children to have and when to have them. As a result they could choose to put off getting married and having a family, and could go to college or have a career instead.

By the end of the 60s women began forming groups to fight for women's rights. Women's groups wanted more equality between men and women, including the right to the same level of education and job opportunities, and to the same rates of pay. Traditionally women were always paid less than men.

They also wanted more nurseries so that women who had young children could go back to work if they wanted. Today, the number of working mothers is three times greater than in the 50s.

The contraceptive pill first arrived in the UK in 1961, but it was only offered to married women. By the 70s single women were taking it too.

> " When I first went to work I spent all the money I earned on shoes and clothes. I didn't get much though. Out of the £2.50 I earned my mum took £2 and I only had 10 shillings, which is 50p in today's money. Women now are much more in control of their lives than they were then. Women were definitely second-class citizens – you weren't put in the pension scheme and you earned less money. "
>
> **Irene, born 1939**

Because of pressure from women's groups the government brought in the Equal Pay Act in 1970, but it was another five years before the Act had any effect.

THE SWINGING SIXTIES

The 60s are remembered as an exciting time when young people rebelled against the beliefs and attitudes of the older generation. Some expressed their ideas by going on marches and protesting. Others created new types of art, fashion and music. And instead of saving their money and settling down when they started working, as their parents would have done, they spent it on music and clothes and having a good time without worrying about the future.

Fashion in the 60s was led by the Mods – fashion-conscious teenagers who spent a fortune on smart, stylish clothes and rode Italian scooters (left).

DOING THINGS DIFFERENTLY

At the age of 19, Prince Charles broke with family tradition by going straight from school to university in 1967 instead of immediately joining the Armed Forces. By the 70s other young people were doing things differently, too. They were dressing differently to their parents, listening to different music and, for the first time, large numbers of them were leaving home to share flats and houses with friends and experiment with different ways of living.

ALL SORTS OF FAMILIES

In the past 60 years changes in the way we do things and the way we think about marriage, divorce, birth control and the rights of women have had a big affect on our family life. Today, families come in many shapes and sizes. There are still lots of traditional married couples with children, but also about one in four children now live with one parent rather than two.

"This is our daughter, my son from my first marriage, John's daughter from his second marriage, and I've no idea who the one on the end is."

Many other children live with parents who are unmarried, or who have married again or are living with different partners. While relationship breakdown remains a painful process, especially for the children, most people are accepting of all the different sorts of families in modern Britain.

"I remember my mother's washing machine. The laundry was loaded in the top and when it was washed you had to pull each piece out with a pair of tongs and feed it through the mangle at the back of the machine to squeeze all the soapy water out. Then all the laundry was rinsed by hand and fed through the mangle again before being hung out to dry. It took all day to do a weekly wash."

Sandra, born 1950

SOMEWHERE TO LIVE

Bomb raids during the war destroyed a lot of Britain's houses and the ones that were left were uncomfortable compared to today. Central heating hardly existed and small houses did not usually have a bathroom or even an indoor toilet. The toilet was in a small brick outhouse at the back of the house or in the back yard. Water for washing was often heated on a stove in the kitchen or by a small gas heater, and people bathed in a tub by the kitchen fire. There were so few houses available that newly-married couples often lived with their parents until they could find a home, or rented a room in someone else's house.

INSTANT HOUSES

The government set out to build new houses as fast as possible. At first, most were temporary houses known as 'prefabs'. Prefabs were made of lightweight metal and timber panels. The parts were pre-made (prefabricated) in factories so they could be quickly put together on site. They were small, boxy, single-storey structures and not very attractive to look at, but they came with built-in luxuries such as a hot-water heater, a bathroom, indoor toilet, and an oven and fridge in the kitchen. They were only meant to last about 10 years, but they were so well-built that a few are still lived in today.

Then & Now

Kitchens
Few kitchens in the 1950s had washing machines, or fridges. People bought just enough fresh food for a day or two and kept it in larders or in boxes called 'food safes'. Clothes were washed by hand and hung up to dry. Freezers, dryers and microwave ovens did not exist. Housework could take hours.

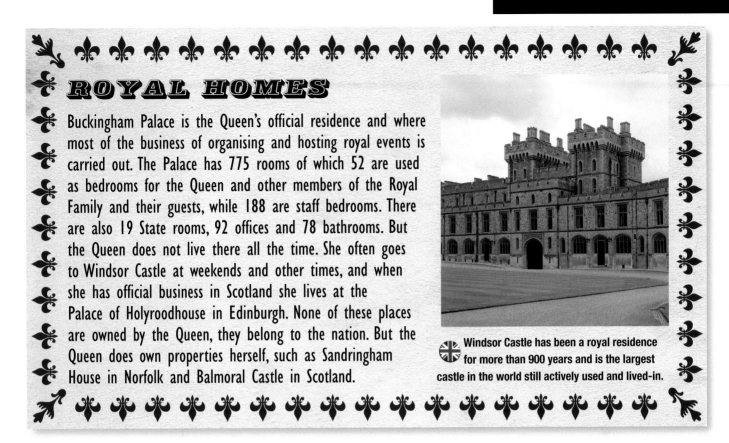

ROYAL HOMES

Buckingham Palace is the Queen's official residence and where most of the business of organising and hosting royal events is carried out. The Palace has 775 rooms of which 52 are used as bedrooms for the Queen and other members of the Royal Family and their guests, while 188 are staff bedrooms. There are also 19 State rooms, 92 offices and 78 bathrooms. But the Queen does not live there all the time. She often goes to Windsor Castle at weekends and other times, and when she has official business in Scotland she lives at the Palace of Holyroodhouse in Edinburgh. None of these places are owned by the Queen, they belong to the nation. But the Queen does own properties herself, such as Sandringham House in Norfolk and Balmoral Castle in Scotland.

Windsor Castle has been a royal residence for more than 900 years and is the largest castle in the world still actively used and lived-in.

BUILDING BLOCKS

In the end, the government built fewer prefabs than they intended. Builders started to use pre-formed slabs of concrete strengthened with steel rods instead of bricks. Like prefabs these could be partly made in factories and put together on site, but, because they were stronger, they could be built into two-storey houses.

They could also be used to build blocks of flats – from 5 floors up to 30 floors high. These 'tower blocks' were especially useful in cities where there was not much land space to build on. However many of them were built too quickly and too cheaply and by the 1970s they were in such a poor condition that people did not want to live in them.

In the 50s, sinks, cookers and cupboards were separate pieces of furniture and were not meant to match each other, unlike today's streamlined, fitted cupboards and built-in machines.

RENTING AND BUYING

Houses and flats built by local government are called council houses and people pay rent to live in them. Until the end of the 60s most people in Britain rented their homes from the council or from landlords. Then more and more people began buying them, especially in the 80s when the government allowed tenants to buy their council houses. Now seven out of ten families own the homes they live in.

HEALTHIER & WEALTHIER

As a nation, Britain is generally healthier and better off than it has ever been. On average, babies born in Britain today can expect to live up to 11 years longer than if they were born in 1950, and 30 years longer than if they were born in 1900. They are also far more likely to get through childhood without dying of some kind of infectious disease. Partly this is due to discoveries of new medicines and improvements in the way illnesses are treated. But it is also because of the huge improvements in public health.

> **"** A story I grew up with was that after my mother gave birth to my older brother at home she nearly died from an infection. It was 1947 and before we had the National Health Service. My father spent all of his savings on buying this miraculous new drug for my mother. It was penicillin and it saved her life. **"**
>
> **Margaret, born 1950**

Then & Now

Living for longer

Life expectancy means the average number of years that someone can expect to live and it is often used as a guide to the general health of a population. In the UK life expectancy has risen over the past 100 years – and it is still rising. In 1900 the life expectancy at birth was 46 years. In 1950 it was 69, and in 2007 it was 80. One in four people now aged under 16 are expected to live to at least 100.

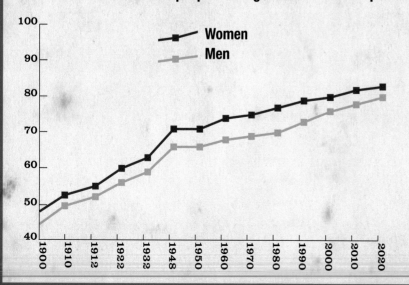

PAYING THE PRICE

In the first half of the 1900s many people lived crowded together in small spaces without proper plumbing or clean water. If you were poor you did not have enough of the right kinds of food to keep you healthy and were more likely to catch infections. Working in factories, mines or farming was often hard, dirty and dangerous and many suffered bad health or injuries through accidents at work.

If you needed a doctor or medicines you usually had to pay — or go without. In any case, few medicines existed that relieved pain, and there were none at all that fought infections until penicillin was mass-produced after World War II. Hospitals were old-fashioned and lacking in medical equipment, and many relied on charity.

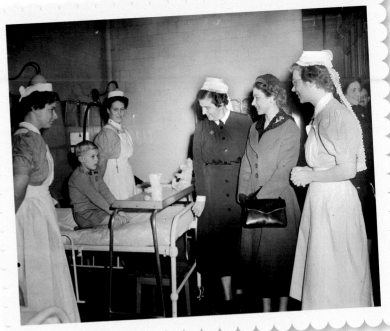

Queen Elizabeth II visits a London hospital in 1954.

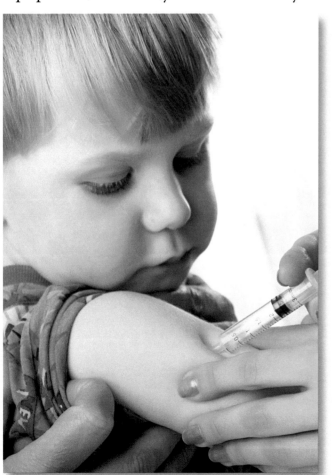

Today free vaccinations protect children from a whole host of diseases.

HEALTH FOR FREE

Things changed dramatically after World War II. In 1948, the government of the time created a new National Health Service. This meant that for the first time medical treatment was freely available to everyone and hospitals were brought under government control.

Children in school were given free health and dental checks, along with their free milk, and they were vaccinated against common childhood diseases such as polio, diphtheria and measles.

In the past 60 years, vaccination programmes have done more than anything to prevent millions of deaths from these diseases and others.

GOVERNMENT CARE

Government regulations were brought in that helped to provide better housing and sanitation, and to protect people from working with dangerous machinery or chemicals. Pensions for retired people were increased, and unemployment and sick pay benefits for those who could not work were made available to all.

CHANGING JOBS

All of these improvements in health and living standards made enormous changes to the lives of most people in Britain, but the cost to the country of providing them has grown equally huge.

During the 60s there were plenty of jobs, rates of pay were rising and more women were at work. With lots of people working the government could raise enough money from the taxes people paid to help cover the costs of the National Health Service and other benefits. People even had extra money to spend on things like household goods, fashion, cars and holidays. But it didn't last — the types of jobs people did were changing. Traditional industries such as coal mining, ship building and engineering were either dying out or being modernised and so needed fewer workers.

HAVES AND HAVE NOTS

As factories and industries closed, thousands of people lost their jobs and some parts of Britain faced massive unemployment, poverty and homelessness. With so many people out of work there was also a big rise in the cost of benefits to help support them.

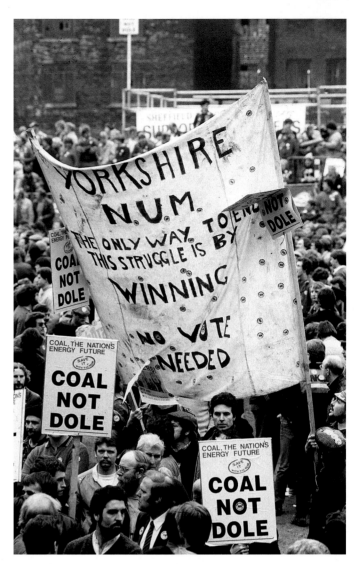

Miners out on strike in 1984. Throughout the 1970s and 80s trade unions and other groups of workers were locked in bitter fights with the government over factory closures, lost jobs and rates of pay.

It was not the same for everyone. For people working in offices, shops, banks and the new computer industry life was pretty good. If you had the right kind of educational qualifications, training and skills you could earn a good wage. If you had little education and no particular skills life could be hard. By the 90s the country was increasingly divided into the 'haves' — people who had jobs and could earn enough money to live reasonably well — and the 'have nots' — those who could not find work, or only very low-paid work, and were increasingly stuck in poverty and relying on benefits.

An office in the 1990s. The widespread use of computers changed the way people worked and the skills they needed.

> " I worked in a factory in the early fifties. We made electrical parts for radios. We started at 7.30 in the morning and finished at 5.30, Monday to Friday, and we worked Saturday mornings. We had one week's holiday a year when the factory closed for a week in the summer. We got paid every Friday afternoon. The money was in a small brown envelope. "
>
> **Grace, born 1923**

THE POVERTY LINE

Today, Britain is still divided. People's wages and the amount of money they have to spend have risen steadily over the past 30 years. At the same time, the population of the UK has increased from 50.3 million in 1951, to 62 million in 2011, and while free health care, old-age pensions and other benefits are available for all, the government struggles to find the money to pay for it.

In 2010 around 2.5 million people were unemployed in the UK, and 13 million people were said to be living below the poverty line. This means that one in five people in the country has less than the minimum level of income needed to pay for the basics of life. For a single person in 2009, for example, this meant having less than £119 a week to spend on food, travel, clothes, heating and so on.

RELATIVE POVERTY

Of course, poverty today does not mean quite the same thing as it did 60 years ago. Back then it might mean not having any shoes to wear, or not getting enough food to eat. Now it is more likely to mean eating cheap but unhealthy food, not going out and having fewer choices than others. But the effects of poverty are the same – you have a lot less than most other people around you.

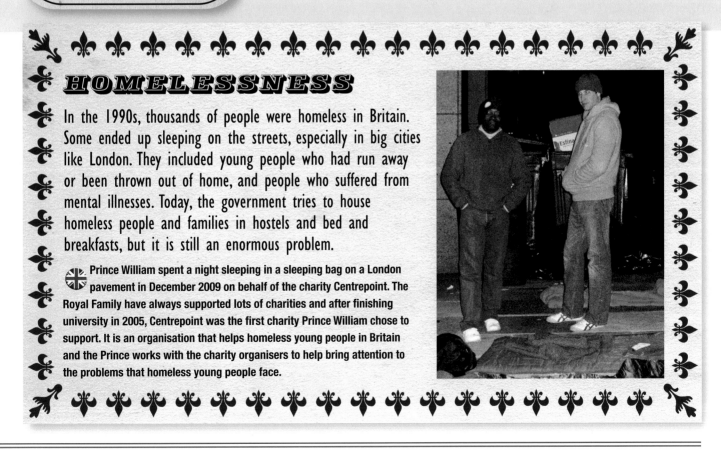

HOMELESSNESS

In the 1990s, thousands of people were homeless in Britain. Some ended up sleeping on the streets, especially in big cities like London. They included young people who had run away or been thrown out of home, and people who suffered from mental illnesses. Today, the government tries to house homeless people and families in hostels and bed and breakfasts, but it is still an enormous problem.

Prince William spent a night sleeping in a sleeping bag on a London pavement in December 2009 on behalf of the charity Centrepoint. The Royal Family have always supported lots of charities and after finishing university in 2005, Centrepoint was the first charity Prince William chose to support. It is an organisation that helps homeless young people in Britain and the Prince works with the charity organisers to help bring attention to the problems that homeless young people face.

GOING PLACES

One of the other major changes to our lives in the past 60 years is the way we travel. In 1950 there were just 2.26 million cars on the roads, roughly one car for every 20 people. By 2009 there were more than 31 million cars, or one for every two people.

People didn't travel that much in the 50s, and if they did they mostly went by train or bus, or they walked. But people were falling in love with the sense of freedom car ownership brought them, and the railways and buses could not compete. Bus use fell steadily from the 50s to the 90s, particularly in the countryside where routes and services were heavily cut. Since 2000, however, more people have begun to travel by bus and long-distance coach again.

TRAVELLING BY TRAIN

The change in train use has been more dramatic. Some improvements were made after the war. For example steam trains were replaced by cleaner, quicker, diesel and electric trains. But gradually more and

 Busy streets in the 50s looked very different to the way they do today. There were no lines or markings painted on the streets and very few road signs. There were no pedestrian crossings either, so people just wandered across the road wherever they felt like it.

> 66 The first car I remember was black and it had running boards on the outside. I must have been about seven or eight and my dad would sometimes let me stand on the running boards and hold on through the open window as he drove slowly up the hill to our house. The front windscreen had a handle on the inside and you could wind it open a little bit. 99
>
> **Bill, born 1950**

more people and goods travelled by road and by the end of the 50s the railways were losing money. Over the next decade hundreds of small, countryside stations were closed. In 1950 there were over 30,000 kilometres of railway lines around the country, but by the early 1990s that had almost halved. But not all the train lines disappeared. Those linking major towns and cities survived and high-speed Intercity trains cut travelling time dramatically. The number of passengers travelling on these trains is now greater than it was in the 1950s.

ON THE ROADS

Otherwise, we mostly travel by car. Cars are comfortable and convenient but they are also noisy, pollute our air and cause accidents. All this car travel has also changed our countryside. The more cars there are, the more roads they need to drive on. The first stretch of motorway was opened in 1958. During the next 10 years 1,000 kilometres of motorways were built and today this has grown to 3,500 kilometres. Altogether there are about 300,000 kilometres of roads in Britain and around three out of four British households have one or more cars.

Then & Now

Up in the air

Before 1950, air travel was relatively slow and very expensive. Long-distance travel usually meant changing planes a number of times and sometimes transferring to trains or boats along the way. In 1935, for example, there was just one Imperial Airways flight from London to Brisbane in Australia per week and the journey took 12½ days. There are now around 25 flights a day from London to Brisbane, and the journey takes about 31 hours.

Concorde, the world's first supersonic (faster than sound) passenger aircraft, began flying in 1969. It took three-and a-half hours to cross the Atlantic – half the time of a normal passenger jet. But it cost too much to keep it in the air and its last flight was on 26th November 2003.

THE ROYAL TRAIN

Sometimes the Royal Family travel by train. When the Queen goes on long journeys around the UK she uses the Royal Train, so that she can sleep on it overnight and hold meetings on it when necessary. But the Royal Train costs about £30,000 per trip, so to save money the Queen and other members of the Royal Family travel on public trains when they can — although always in a first-class carriage. The first Royal Train was used by Queen Victoria in 1842. The present version came into use in 1977 for the Silver Jubilee tours.

Prince Charles climbs on board the Royal Train in 2010 at the start of a five-day tour of the towns and cities between Glasgow and London.

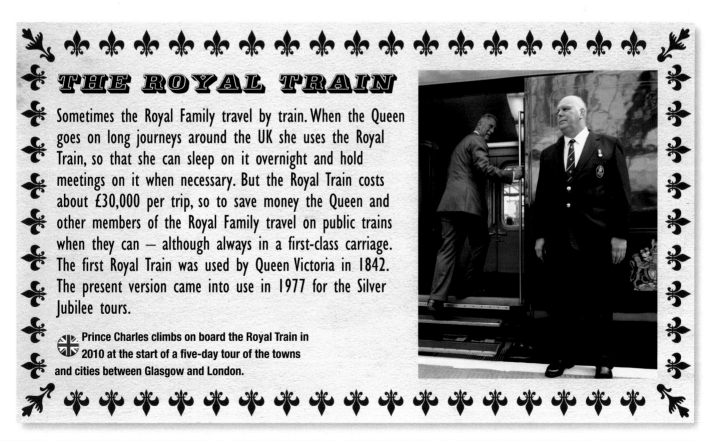

IT'S GOOD TO TALK

Telephones were slow to take off in Britain. They had been invented in the 1870s, but 100 years later barely half of all homes in the UK had a phone.

Getting a telephone at home could take months and it was expensive. You had to rent one from the General Post Office (GPO) and pay for a line to be connected, as well as paying for the calls. Things changed in the 1980s. The phone services became known as British Telecom (BT) and were separated from the GPO, and other phone companies were allowed to compete with BT's services. As a result the telephone service became cheaper and more efficient and by the end of the 90s nearly all households had a phone.

TALKING AND WALKING

But the big difference came with mobile phones. Mobile radio phones existed in the 60s, but they were big and bulky and were mostly used in cars and other vehicles. The kind of mobile we are more familiar with appeared in the second half of the 80s. It could be held in one hand but it was still as large and as heavy as a house brick. Nevertheless it was an instant hit with wealthy business people.

Since then, mobiles have become smaller, lighter and far more powerful. There are now more mobile phones in Britain than there are people and almost every home has one or more mobile phones as well as a landline.

In 1985 the first mobile phones were awkward to carry, soon ran out of battery power, and the only thing you could do with them was make phone calls.

Today's mobiles are a fraction of the size and can be used to send emails and text messages, take photos, play games or watch movies – and make phone calls.

USING COMPUTERS

Mobile phones are not the only things to get smaller and more powerful. The fastest and probably biggest technological revolution in the past 60 years has been the development of computers. The first computers were built by the US and British military during World War II. These machines were so big they filled an entire room, and were so expensive that only the military and large universities could afford to build them.

The first digital computer, ENIAC (above), filled an entire room. Today's computers are no bigger than a book (left) but are far more powerful.

By the 60s and 70s, computers were being used by businesses, but they still filled entire rooms and were very slow by today's standards. Then along came the microchip in 1971. Suddenly computers became small enough to sit on a desktop.

By the end of the 70s the first personal computers came on sale. To begin with they were sold as kits that you had to assemble yourself, but ready-made computers soon followed. Among them was the Apple II, Apple's first complete computer, which came with a computer game and colour graphics — when it was connected to a television set. Today, three out of four households in Britain own a computer and many have more than one.

THE QUEEN'S PHONE

It has been reported that Queen Elizabeth got her first mobile phone in 2001 as a present from her son, Prince Andrew. Although she occasionally finds mobile phones annoying and has banned her staff from using them while they are on duty, she has apparently become rather attached to her phone which she uses mostly to keep in touch with members of her family. In fact, the Queen appears to be keen on keeping up with new technology. She uses email and has a Facebook page and an Apple iPad. She reportedly sent her first tweet in 2014.

The way we live today is different in so many ways to how it was when Queen Elizabeth first came to the throne, from the huge range of computers and electronic gadgets we all depend on, to the types of food we eat and the way we shop. Most people's lives have got busier, faster and more varied and we have more choices than ever before in what we wear, buy, read, listen to and do.

THE WAY WE LIVE

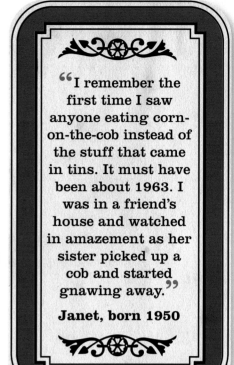

"I remember the first time I saw anyone eating corn-on-the-cob instead of the stuff that came in tins. It must have been about 1963. I was in a friend's house and watched in amazement as her sister picked up a cob and started gnawing away."

Janet, born 1950

A CHANGING POPULATION

Even the people of Britain are more varied than ever before. In the first half of the 1900s the population of the UK was mostly made up of those born in England, Ireland, Scotland and Wales, along with a sprinkling of people from Europe and other parts of the world. During the war that began to change when large numbers of people fled to the UK to escape the violence and persecution that was happening in the rest of Europe.

Immediately after the war Britain was short of workers and the government invited people to come and work here. They came from Europe and from parts of the Empire, and later from the newly-named Commonwealth countries.

In 1948 the British troop ship *Empire Windrush* arrived in Britain carrying the first group of immigrants from Jamaica since the war. Many of them had fought as British soldiers during the war and were returning to Britain to take up the government's offer of jobs.

Some of these immigrant workers stayed for a while and then went home again. Others made the UK their home. At the same time, some people left to go to countries such as Australia, Canada, New Zealand and South Africa.

This flow of people into and out of the UK has continued ever since. People move here from all over the world — for work, or education, or to escape dangers or poverty

The Duchess of Cornwall and Prince Charles visiting Brixton Market in London. Brixton Market has been a centre for the black community in London since the 50s and it is famous for the wide range of Afro-Caribbean and other international foods it sells.

in other lands. They bring with them their skills, their languages, their arts, their ideas and their customs — many of which have influenced our way of life.

FAVOURITE FOOD

Probably one of the most obvious ways in which immigration has changed our society is through the food we eat. In the 50s British food tended to be stodgy and rather bland. It relied heavily on bread, potatoes, pastries and pies and was intended to fill you up rather than be exciting to eat.

Once rationing was over, meat or sometimes fish would be served up with every main meal. To eat a meal of just vegetables was considered a bit peculiar. Vegetables and fruit were largely limited to what could be grown locally and in season — so strawberries were only available for a few weeks in the summer, for example.

ROYAL FOOD

In 1953 a dish known as Coronation Chicken was specially invented to appeal to the foreign guests at the Queen's coronation lunch. It was made from pieces of cold cooked chicken mixed with a bright yellow sauce made from mayonnaise, cream and curry powder and was served with a salad of rice and peas. It is not as popular today as it once was, but can still sometimes be found as a filling in ready-made sandwiches.

TINS OF THINGS

In the 50s tinned food was very popular, especially foods such as tinned ham, peas, peaches and mixed fruit salad. Few families owned a fridge, so fresh food didn't keep for long and frozen food was not available. Rice was usually only eaten as rice pudding, and pasta was mostly unknown apart from macaroni, which was put into soups or used to make macaroni cheese.

Then & Now

New money

In 1971 Britain changed its money from pounds (£), shillings (s) and pence (d), to a decimal currency made up of just pounds (£) and pence (d). The old money divided up as 12 pennies to a shilling, and 20 shillings to a pound. The new currency was much easier – just 100 pennies to a pound. Even so, lots of people found it hard to get used to the new currency.

'FOREIGN' FOODS

By the 60s and 70s things were changing fast. Chinese, Indian and Italian restaurants were opening up in every town and city. American-style hot dogs and hamburgers followed, as did Greek and Turkish restaurants. People started experimenting with cooking different recipes at home, and as the demand for 'foreign' ingredients grew more shops began to sell them. By the 90s, Indian curries, Italian pastas and pizzas and Chinese stir-frys were normal meals in many households. For those people short on time or cooking skills, supermarkets developed a range of pre-prepared meals influenced by foods from around the world.

Left: Spam is a pre-cooked canned meat that was first made in the USA in the mid-1930s and is now sold all over the world. During and after the war Spam was popular because it was cheap and could be used in lots of ways. Many people see it as a symbol of the poor quality of British food in the 50s, although some still love it.

Right: Today, foods from all over the world, like this dish of Indian curry and rice, are pre-cooked and packaged up so they can be re-heated in an instant.

SMALL AND LOCAL

Even buying food is a totally different experience today. In the 50s most shops were small and local, and specialised in selling just one type of thing — bread came from the bakers, meat from the butchers, flour, sugar and other dried goods from the grocer, and so on. People bought small amounts and shopped often, maybe three or four times a week, and waited to be served at a counter.

SUPER SHOPS

The first few self-service shops, where you picked your own goods off the shelf, began to appear at the end of the 40s, and the first supermarkets arrived in the early 50s. They were far smaller than they are today, but they still allowed you to buy all of your food in one place.

Every small group of streets had a corner shop in the 50s, where local people could buy everything from tea and bacon to matches, string and a bag of sweets. Usually the shop owner lived above the shop.

Supermarkets were pretty much an instant success and as they grew bigger they could stock an even greater variety of goods. Eventually they became too big to be built in the high street and by the 1980s vast hypermarkets were appearing on the outskirts of towns that sold everything from food, to electrical goods, household furniture, and clothes.

HOW ABOUT SOME MARITAL COUNSELLING, HON? SHOULD WE GRAB SOME WHILE WE'RE IN THIS AISLE?

NO, WE'RE FINE ON THAT.

"I remember when they opened a big supermarket superstore outside our town in the early 90s. I couldn't believe how big it was or that you could buy clothes alongside your food shopping."

Sam, born 1980

WELL DRESSED

Clothing was far more formal in the 50s than it is now. When women wanted to look smart they always wore a hat and gloves – even with a summer dress. It was a style the Queen was famous for right from the start, and still wears today.

Men wore suits or a tailored jacket and trousers, with a tie and sometimes a waistcoat. Children were often dressed in similar clothes to their parents, except that young boys wore short trousers and girls wore socks rather than stockings. Teenagers did not have their own clothing style. Instead most young people tried to look as much like adults as possible.

Things were changing fast, though, and with the arrival of American jazz and rock 'n' roll, teenagers started to follow fashions that had nothing to do with their parents. Girls wore full skirts with lots of stiff petticoats underneath them so the skirts flared out, while some boys dressed as Teddy boys in narrow 'drainpipe' trousers and long fitted jackets. Boys were also beginning to wear denim jeans for the first time in the UK.

MINIS, BELL-BOTTOMS, BOOTS AND CHAINS

The 60s was a fantastic time for fashion in the UK, and for the first time it was driven by teenagers. Suddenly all sorts of styles, colours and new materials became available.

THE ROYAL FASHION ICON

Princess Diana was one of the most photographed women in the world and unlike many of the older members of the Royal Family she proved that she could be a leader of fashion as well. At first, Diana dressed in a very traditional way, often wearing clothes that looked rather dowdy and too old for her. But she quickly developed her own style, which was modern and glamorous. Soon other women were copying her clothes, her handbags and her hairstyles.

Right: Princess Diana arrives at the British Fashion Awards in 1989 in London.

Left: Punk fashion in the mid-70s featured clothes held together with safety pins and chains, worn with big boots and extreme hairstyles.

Fashion designers like Mary Quant became household names. When Quant introduced her 'mini-skirts' in the mid-60s many older people were shocked, but the young loved them.

Since then fashions have changed and changed again, although some things like jeans and short skirts never seem to go away. The end of the 60s and early 70s saw the rise of the 'hippie' look, with long hair for boys as well as girls, swirly-patterned t-shirts and flared, bell-bottom trousers.

Punk fashion set out to shock the older generation all over again, this time with ripped clothes and chains, spiky hair styles and lots of make-up. By the 80s this had mostly given way to a more glamorous style that was not led by teenagers but by young adults who had plenty of money. Sports clothing also became fashionable even for people who never do any kind of sport. Now fashions change from year to year. There are no rules any longer about what you can or cannot wear. Instead people choose the clothes they feel suit them best.

AT THE CINEMA

The 50s was not a great time for having fun. Most people's lives were quiet and orderly, and rather dull. People were careful with their money and if they went out it was usually to the local cinema to see the latest glamorous Hollywood film from the USA. Otherwise families stayed at home in the evening to listen to the radio, or to watch television — if they had one. Most women sewed or knitted clothes for themselves and their families, and at weekends men washed the car and grew vegetables in their garden.

At the beginning of the 50s almost every town had at least one cinema. In those days each cinema only had one screen, but the films changed regularly and there were a number of showings each day. Cinema tickets were not expensive and there was always a short film and a newsreel before the main feature film. Children's films were shown on Saturday mornings. For many people, the cinema kept them up-to-date with the news and with the latest fashion styles, dances, make-up and hairstyles.

 Children queue up outside a London cinema while they wait to watch Saturday morning movies in 1957.

In 1969 the first TV documentary was made about the Royal family. Cameras were allowed to follow them around and film them at home. When it was made it was watched by 23 million people, but at the end of that year it was withdrawn from public viewing.

WHAT'S ON THE BOX?

By the middle of the 50s, however, television was taking over and cinema audiences were falling. In competition with the BBC, ITV began broadcasting in 1955 showing a mixture of programmes and advertising, and in 1964 the BBC launched a second channel, BBC Two.

The mixture of news, documentaries, dramas, films, comedies and children's programmes had something for everyone. Shows like *Sunday Night at the London Palladium* kept the whole family glued to the set. In the 1980s, home video players allowed people to watch whatever they wanted through their television screen, and 'the box' became the main source of entertainment.

In recent years, even though television still dominates most people's leisure time, going out to the movies has regained some of its popularity. Large multi-screen cinemas offer lots of choice and the use of special effects such as 3-D and IMAX can only really be enjoyed on the big screen.

THE FIRST SOAP

In 1954 the BBC showed the first ever British soap opera, called *The Grove Family*. It ran for three years and had about 220 episodes. It was fairly tame by today's standards but its success paved the way for all those that followed.

FROM BALLROOM TO THE BEATLES

Aside from the cinema, the other place to go for a good night out in the 50s was to the local ballroom or dance hall. Going to a dance was the best way for young single men and women to meet, and most towns had at least one dance hall that held dances two or three times a week. Older couples danced the tango and the cha-cha-cha to music played by dance bands. But younger people preferred to jive and dance to rock 'n' roll music.

The 60s changed the face of popular music. The big American rock 'n' roll stars of the 50s, like Bill Haley and Elvis Presley played the music that other people wrote for them. In the 60s hundreds of young British rock and pop groups started appearing. They wrote and performed their own songs as well as other people's. Many of them sank without a trace, but some, like the Beatles and the Rolling Stones, became superstars.

In 1959 an American singer called Chubby Checker released a song called 'The Twist', and started a worldwide craze for a new way of dancing.

A record player from the 60s with a stack of single records. When each record had finished playing, the 'needle' arm swung out and worked a mechanism so that the next record could drop down.

Then & Now

Music makers

Listening to music at home 60 years ago usually meant buying records and playing them on a record player or maybe your parents' gramophone – a large boxy piece of furniture that was both a record player and a radio. By the 1960s record players had become 'portable', but were still the size and weight of a small packed suitcase. Things improved in the 70s, when tape cassettes allowed you to record a mixture of songs onto one tape that played for 90 minutes. But by the 90s, tapes had been replaced by longer-lasting CDs with better sound quality.

FESTIVAL TIME

The first big outdoor folk, rock and pop music festivals at places such as Woburn Abbey, the Isle of Wight, and Glastonbury started happening in the late 60s and early 70s. Hordes of young people camped out in fields to watch bands play. Back then, most of the people who went to these festivals were hippies, but music festivals of all sorts are now a major part of the summer music scene, whether it is classical music, jazz, rock or pop.

Right: Prince Charles and Princess Diana with Bob Geldof at the opening of the Live Aid concert at Wembley Stadium in London, in 1985.

You can still buy records today, but many people listen to music, downloaded as files from the Internet, through MP3 players like this one, that let you carry thousands of songs in your pocket.

LIVE AID

In 1985, Live Aid made history by linking together two simultaneous concerts, one in London and the other in Philadelphia in the USA, and broadcasting them live all over the world to raise money for starving people in Ethiopia. Performers at the concerts included some of the biggest stars in the music world. More than 72,000 people were in the audience at Wembley Stadium and about 100,000 were at Philadelphia, while millions more watched it on television. The concert in London raised over £1 million, and around the world £30 million was raised overall.

The 70s was also a great time for going to clubs called discoteques and dancing to a rhythmic, electronic sound known as disco music. The music often came from records played by DJs rather than live performers. During the 80s and 90s, the word 'disco' went out of fashion and instead people talked about dance clubs, 'house music' and 'raves'. Today there are hundreds of dance clubs around the country — each playing its own style of music and attracting its own fans.

 Camping holidays in France were popular in the 1970s.

BY THE SEASIDE

Having a holiday in the 50s was most likely to mean a visit to the British seaside. You might go just for a day, or for a week and stay in a bed-and-breakfast or a small hotel. Seaside towns like Blackpool were popular because if the weather was bad there were games arcades and cinemas, and other things to do.

Many liked holiday camps, too. They had existed before the war but really took off in the 50s and 60s. Camps such as Butlin's had chalets for people to stay in. They had swimming pools, ballrooms, restaurants and games rooms. They also laid on entertainment for adults and children so everyone could be kept busy.

As more people got their own cars they began to explore other parts of Britain as well. In August, the roads leading to Devon and Cornwall became one long traffic jam. An adventurous few put their cars on a ferry and crossed the Channel to countries like France and Belgium. Caravans became fashionable, and caravan parks sprang up everywhere.

PACKAGED UP

In the 60s, the development of the package holiday put a serious dent in the popularity of the British seaside. Why sit on a deckchair on a cold British beach when you could be lying on the sand in sunny Spain? Package holidays put the cost of the flight and the hotel all together into one affordable package and made foreign travel available to many people for the first time – and thousands jumped at it.

" It says here... ....a typically quiet Spanish fishing village ! "

Budget airlines arrived in the 70s. These companies offered low-price air tickets by doing away with the 'extras' that regular airlines offered on a flight, such as free meals and drinks. Instead of taking a package holiday people discovered they could organise their own holidays abroad – buying a flight to somewhere and choosing their own hotel. For many, the notion of 'travel' rather than 'holiday' became more enticing – and the further they could go, and the more exotic, the better.

People now go on holiday to almost anywhere in the world, and it is not unusual to take two or even three holiday breaks in a year, although at least one of them is likely to be taken in the UK. Activity holidays are increasingly popular, but lots of people still choose a package holiday in the sun. And you can still sit on a deckchair at Blackpool beach and eat an ice cream.

Activity holidays, which involve sports such as skiing, diving and cycling, are increasingly fashionable.

"My parents took me on my first trip abroad to Greece in 1980 on a package holiday. It was really exciting going on a plane to another country – none of my friends had been on a plane. Now my holidays are planned with the Internet so we can get exactly what we want."

Laura, born 1973

LOOKING AHEAD

Over the last 60 years Britain and other countries have burnt vast quantities of coal, oil and gas in power stations to produce the electricity that we rely on. Now we are looking towards other 'greener' forms of power generation such as wind power (above), solar energy and wave power.

The speed and breadth of change in the past 60 years has been greater than ever before in history. In general, people in Britain today are healthier, better fed, housed and dressed, and have more money in their pockets than their grandparents could ever have imagined. This is not true for all, certainly, and there is still much poverty and hardship in the UK, but nevertheless life has improved enormously.

However, all this progress has come at a cost that we are only now beginning to recognise. Like other developed nations, much of our wealth as a country had depended on the growth of industry and the use of machines. The waste products from these industries and machines, and from some of the goods and materials they produce, have been slowly building up and poisoning our air, water and land.

Yet the scientific discoveries of the past hundred years that brought us to this point also offer us the best chance we have of finding solutions to these problems, and many people believe that it is the scientists of the future that will find them.

IN THE FUTURE

We cannot know for sure what will happen in the future, except that things will continue to change. We will probably all have to think more carefully about the machines we use, the way we travel, the food we eat and the things that we buy. It is also clear that we can no longer see ourselves as separate from the rest of the world. Today, every country is linked together, through banking, trade and through travel and tourism.

One side effect of being healthier is that as a nation we are growing older – literally. In 2007 there were fewer under-16-year-olds in the population than there were people drawing their old-age pension, and this gap is expected to continue growing for at least the next few decades. The cost to the country of the NHS and pension benefits will continue to rise, and with fewer young people to support them older people will have to carry on working for longer, and retirement at 60 or 65 will no longer be an option.

A LINK TO THE PAST

The Queen has been there throughout all the major events of the past 60 years. She and the Royal Family represent our link to that past, to our history and to our ancient traditions. Yet as our lives and our ways of looking at the world change, so the lives of the Royal Family change with us – as they have throughout the Queen's reign.

More than any other monarch before her, the daily life and work of the Queen and her family has become open to the public view. It is available for all to see on her official website, and she and the other members of her family are more involved in public concerns than ever before. To many British people, the Royal family are symbols of both our past and our present. No matter what our future is, it is likely we will all be part of it together.

The marriage of Kate Middleton and Prince William, who is second-in-line to the throne, shows how much royal life has changed over the past 60 years. Traditionally most royal partners are either members of royalty themselves or belong to the aristocracy, whereas Kate is an ordinary member of the public.

TIMELINE

1922 The BBC begins broadcasting national radio programmes.

1926 Princess Elizabeth is born to the Duke and Duchess of York, who later became King George VI and Queen Elizabeth.

1930 Princess Margaret, the Queen's sister, is born. (Dies in 2002.)

1936 King George V dies and his oldest son Edward becomes king, but then gives up the throne. His brother the Duke of York becomes King George VI.

The first television programmes are broadcast by the BBC, but television is halted during World War II and only BBC radio continues.

1939–1945 World War II.

1944 The Education Act makes all state secondary schools free and raises the school leaving age to 15.

1945 The United Nations (UN) is founded.

BBC television starts broadcasting again.

1946 The first passenger flights leave London Heathrow Airport.

1947 Princess Elizabeth marries Prince Philip of Greece and Denmark, now known as the Duke of Edinburgh. (In the years following, the Queen and Prince Philip have four children: Prince Charles, born in 1948, Princess Anne, born in 1950, Prince Andrew, born in 1960, and Prince Edward, born in 1964.)

The Co-op is running the first self-service food shops in Britain.

1948 The National Health Service is launched.

The Olympic Games are held in London. These are the first Games to be held since 1936.

The SS *Empire Windrush* brings the first post-war Caribbean immigrants to the UK.

1949 King George VI becomes the first Head of the Commonwealth of Nations.

1950 Sainsbury opens its first self-service store.

1951 The Festival of Britain is held.

Lyons Tea Company becomes the first business in the UK to use a computer.

1952 King George VI dies and his daughter becomes Queen Elizabeth II.

1953 The coronation of Queen Elizabeth II is held in Westminster Abbey.

1954 Rationing comes to an end in Britain.

Tesco opens its first self-service supermarket.

1955 The first commercial television station, ITV, begins broadcasting.

First polio vaccinations.

1958 The Campaign for Nuclear Disarmament (CND) is founded.

First stretch of motorway opens, later forming part of the M6.

1960 The first episode of 'Coronation Street' is broadcast on TV.

1961 The contraceptive pill becomes available to the public for the first time in the UK.

1962 The Beatles have their first hit record, called 'Love Me Do'.

1963 First vaccinations against measles become available.

1964 The BBC launches its second channel – BBC Two.

1965 Mini-skirts come into fashion for the first time.

1966 England wins the football World Cup.

1967 The first colour television programmes are broadcast by the BBC.

1968 British people demonstrate against the US war in Vietnam.

Women workers at the Ford car factory in Dagenham strike over equal pay. The strike leads to the Equal Pay Act of 1970.

1969 First official flight of Concorde – the world's first supersonic passenger jet.

The Divorce Law Reform Act makes it simpler to get a divorce in the UK.

The death penalty for murder is abolished in Britain.

1971 British money is decimalised.

The first Women's Liberation march in the UK is held in London.

In the USA, the first email message is sent using an early version of the Internet, called ARPANET.

1972 Coal miners go on strike for seven weeks over pay. Because of power cuts the government brings in a three-day working week to save electricity.

1973 The UK joins the EEC (now known as the European Union or EU).

First hand-held mobile phone is produced by Motorola in the US.

1976 Apple I, the first Apple personal computer, goes on sale in the USA.

1977 The Queen's Silver Jubilee is held to celebrate her 25 years on the throne.

1979 Transport workers go on strike, including truck drivers, rubbish collectors and ambulance drivers.

1981 Prince Charles marries Lady Diana Spencer. (They have two children, Prince William, born 1982, and Prince Harry, born 1984.)

1983 The ARPANET is divided into the MILNET, for military use only, and the ARPANET for non-military use. In 1995 the ARPANET is renamed the Internet.

1984 Coal miners strike again against closure of the coal mines, but this time the strike fails and pits start closing.

1985 The Live Aid concerts are held in London and Philadelphia.

1992 Prince Charles and Princess Diana officially separate and are divorced in 1996.

The UN's first Earth Summit is held, in Brazil.

1994 The Channel Tunnel is opened between Britain and France.

1997 Princess Diana is killed in a car crash.

2002 The Queen's Golden Jubilee celebrates her 50 years on the throne.

2005 Prince Charles marries Mrs Camilla Parker Bowles.

2011 Prince William marries Kate Middleton.

2012 The Queen's Diamond Jubilee celebrates her 60 years on the throne.

London hosts the 2012 Summer Olympic Games.

2015 Queen Elizabeth II becomes Britain's longest reigning monach.

FURTHER INFORMATION & WEBSITES

www.bbc.co.uk/history/british/modern
A collection of articles on 'The Making of Modern Britain' on the BBC's History website. Also see the 'History for Kids' section.

www.britishpathe.com
British Pathé produced all the cinema newsreels from 1896 to 1976. This website allows you to view video clips of the news as it happened.

www.mylearning.org
A website for learners and teachers inspired by museum, library and archive collections in Yorkshire and the North West of England. Click on 'Subjects' to find history topics, or 'Age Group' to find material suitable for your needs.

www.nationalarchives.gov.uk
The National Archives is the official government body that looks after the country's historical and public records dating back for hundreds of years. It's quite a complicated website, but if you click on 'Education' you will find some wonderful photos, facts, original documents and other information from 1066 to the present day.

http://primaryhomeworkhelp.co.uk
A really interesting and useful website from Woodlands Junior School in Kent. Click on the 'History' section for lots of good information about Britain during and after World War II.

www.royal.gov.uk
The official website of the British Monarchy has loads of information about Queen Elizabeth II and the other members of the Royal Family, as well as all the kings and queens of the past.

Note to parents and teachers: Every effort has been made by the Publishers to ensure that these websites are suitable for children, that they are of the highest educational value, and that they contain no inappropriate or offensive material. However, because of the nature of the Internet, it is impossible to guarantee that the contents of these sites will not be altered. We strongly advise that Internet access is supervised by a responsible adult.

INDEX